Do All Things Through CHRIST

A Devotional Consideration of Philippians

Howard Rudolph

ISBN 978-1-67815-3861

To All the Saints
"In CHRIST JESUS"

A devotional yes. As what is gained spiritually if we consider the Holy Scriptures as merely historical facts written by earthly man? Or should we instead look deeply into what THE HOLY SPIRIT – THE AUTHOR of all Scripture is seeking to teach and instruct us, for our lives while we are here on this earth! Using THE HOLY SPIRIT filled Apostle Paul as a great example?!

THE HOLY SPIRIT, WHO indwells the born-again Christian, resides within you, to be, you're TEACHER of TRUTH, convict you of sin, testifies of CHRIST, reveals THE FATHER and is your COMFORTER. As THE SPIRIT has a message, -
"To all the saints IN CHRIST."

A Devotional consideration of
Philippians.

THE HOLY SPIRIT revealing to us, the awesome power that is shared to those who seek an on-going abiding relationship with their LORD.

In Philippians 4:13 it is summed up, -
"I can do all things through CHRIST WHO strengthens me."
A devotional study in Philippians may, change   and empower you to such 'Strength.'

Howard Rudolph

Contents

Chapter		Page
1	Setting the stage	6
2	Grace and Peace in you	8
3	You are remembered for what	11
4	The Good Work continues in you	15
5	Love deepened by Application	19
6	Things which happen	27
7	Rejoice in the things that happen	32
8	CHRIST Magnified for you	35
9	To Live is CHRIST	40
10	Worthy of the Gospel	44
11	Esteem others Better	50
12	A Servant's Mind	54
13	JESUS CHRIST is LORD	56
14	Work out your own salvation	61
15	All seek their own	65
16	Little known man of faith	69
17	Brethren Beware	73
18	May I Gain CHRIST	76
19	Press on for CHRIST	81
20	Stand Fast in THE LORD	84
21	THE LORD is at hand	89
22	Meditate on these things	92
23	Do all things through CHRIST	94
24	Sweet – Smelling Aroma	96
25	Your Needs Supplied	101
	Other Books by Howard Rudolph	103

1

Setting the Scene

Please note, as we study this portion of ALMIGHTY GOD'S WORD, that there is no clear divisions as in many other Scriptures.

Many scholars select certain statements as, 'key verses.' However, I believe that the opening statement via THE HOLY SPIRIT in verse 1 is most important – setting the heavenly scene, for all that is going to be declared to us –

"To all the saints in CHRIST JESUS."

As the statement, *"all saints In CHRIST"* does not refer to all Christians, but to the select few who continue, shall we say, they are 'on-going' - that is the ones who continue to study, worship and increase in their knowledge of JESUS CHRIST their SAVIOR and LORD. Fully knowing and realizing that they have the very, 'presence of CHRIST within them.' Therefore, "IN" CHRIST.

Yes, all born-again Christians have THE HOLY SPIRIT dwelling within. However, not all Christians continue in fellowship with their LORD.

As un-confessed sin grieves THE HOLY SPIRIT. If 'non-confession continues,' THE SPIRIT is quenched. THE SPIRIT continues to dwell within, but is displaced and set aside because of the un-confessed sin. Leaving such completely - 'On their own' as they venture forth, limited to their own logical resources and knowledge.

But the 'Power from Above' is not available as a heavenly resource!

This resource is 'Part of the born-again Christians life,' who continue on, growing, in their relationship with THE LORD of GLORY, becoming mature and confessing their sin. Have the knowledge and understand that THE HOLY SPIRIT dwells within, as such they have become the 'inner sanctuary' of THE LORD. Meaning the Most Holy Place. 1 Corinthians 3:16, KJV, -

"Know ye not that ye are the temple of GOD, and that THE SPIRIT of GOD dwelleth in you? **Therefore, -**
"In CHRIST."

To such believing 'on-going' Christians, THE HOLY SPIRIT is going to challenge us in a number of areas of our lives in CHRIST.

THE SPIRIT has declared to us, -

"The things which happened to me have actually turned out for the furtherance of the gospel." 1:12

Question, have the things that occurred in your life, resulted in others seeking and coming into the knowledge of CHRIST? Or has your actions and reactions, and your life style, turned them away, even fleeing from your presence? And your beliefs?

2

Grace and Peace is yours

Philippians 1:1-2,

"Paul and Timothy, bondservants of JESUS CHRIST, to all the saints in CHRIST JESUS who are in Philippi, with the bishops and deacons: Grace to you and peace from GOD our FATHER and THE LORD JESUS CHRIST."

This is a devotional Bible study, meaning = Not just checking into the historical Biblical Truths, nor is it a study of Paul's life. And not taking ourselves back in time. But grasping the Scriptural Truths, from THE HOLY SPIRIT into our innermost beings. Then, 'applying' these Scriptural Truths into our daily lives, as we go-forth today. Understanding that THE HOLY SPIRIT IS 'The Author' has and is ministering to born-again Christians (Saints) for the past 2,000 plus years. And will continue until our LORD calls us home at the Glorious Rapture.

Please know and understand that, 'Saints' refers to those whom JESUS CHRIST has chosen and called to HIMSELF! As THE SPIRIT has written for us, what THE LORD JESUS says, in John 15:16, *"Ye have not chosen ME, but I have chosen you; and ordained you, that ye should go and bring forth fruit, and that your fruit should remain ..."*

This message, known as 'Philippians,' was first directed to the assembly there at Philippi.

Then further, reaching to all, "The Saints" in CHRIST JESUS, throughout the entire world! That is to those who are sanctified and consecrated. The 'set apart' ones, who are looking toward THE LORD'S coming for them at the Rapture. Including such believing ones, of today, and continuing until that Glorious Day of HIS appearing for us in the clouds.

The Holy Scriptures, we refer to as the Bible, is ALMIGHTY GOD'S Living WORD!

The 'Living WORD' via THE HOLY SPIRIT, is able to minister to you. Regardless if you are a new convert requiring basic, foundational understanding, or a mature Christian being fully grounded and settled not only in the foundational Truths. But have gone on gaining knowledge of doctrinal truths and are able to share them with others. Such grounded one's is to whom THE HOLY SPIRIT has first addressed. Then, to the bishops. The title bishop is in reference to 'all those' who are in an overseeing position, as elders and teaching and presenting the truths of JESUS CHRIST. As well to those whose minister to the needs of the assemblies, the deacons.

THE HOLY SPIRIT is making it very clear that 'all' Christians are exactly at the same spiritual level in THE LORD JESUS CHRIST. The elders and deacons are 'not over or above' but are the chosen one's going-forth as servants, to instruct.

Such is the opening declaration, *"Paul and Timothy, bondservants of JESUS CHRIST."*

Bondservants, THE SPIRIT not seeing them as overlords, but presenting them who were purchased at an awful price, by THE LORD. Now their pleasure is to do the duty set before them – 'The proclamation of the Good News the gospel of JESUS CHRIST, as chosen and set apart servants of CHRIST. For HIS use, HIS Plans and HIS Purposes.

Thus the message from THE SPIRIT is, "Grace and Peace" from GOD THE FATHER and THE LORD JESUS CHRIST. Such addressing comes only from the Heavenly Author, THE HOLY SPIRIT, WHO represents, GOD THE FATHER and THE LORD JESUS CHRIST!

As we study through the Scriptures, we realize that our LORD has blessed us with unmerited favor (grace). For we are not cable of earning the grace that we have been so richly blessed with.

It is all only possible via the Sacrifice of JESUS CHRIST in our place washing away our sins, by HIS Precious Blood for us. Following this blessing of grace – forgiveness of all our sins, we have peace with GOD, as we are now no longer under HIS condemnation.

But have been elevated into citizens of Heaven's Glory! Wonder what the result would be if (if) we demonstrated our heavenly citizenship, via ALMIGHTY GOD'S Grace throughout our daily lives, what a difference it would show to this dark unbelieving world who so desperately needs to hear, and see THE LIGHT OF THE WORLD – JESUS!

3

You are Remembered for what?

Philippians 1:3-5,

"I thank my GOD upon every remembrance of you, always in every prayer of mine making request for you all with joy, for your fellowship in the gospel from the first day until now,"

Question, what is 'held in remembrance of us' by others and especially our LORD?

Our LORD gives us a great example, using HIS servant Paul.

The apostle Paul was a giant in and of the faith in JESUS CHRIST! As such THE SPIRIT (The Author) demonstrated at the very opening, "Paul and Timothy" – the spiritual giant Paul, is deeply associated with, the young believer Timothy at his side.

Teaching us that we are to 'reach out' embracing and encouraging young believers in JESUS CHRIST! Not setting them aside until they become filled with knowledge and obedience. No!
Instead, bring them along, providing those with opportunities to not only observe, but to apply, their

voices. Thus venturing forth with the good news of the gospel.

Instructing them, that they are not to rely, on man nor his teachings, but on THE HOLY SPIRIT and HIS ministering first to and in them! That THE HOLY SPIRIT 'may minister through them.'

This is part of our participating fellowship in presenting the gospel. And we are to rejoice with one another as we together go forth.

This is what our LORD instructed us to do. Matthew 28:18,

"JESUS came and spoke to them, saying, "All authority has been given to ME in heaven and on earth. Go therefore and make disciples of all nations, baptizing them in THE NAME of THE FATHER and of THE SON and of THE HOLY SPIRIT, teaching them to observe all things that I have commanded you; and lo, I AM with you always, even to the end of the age." Amen.

Disciples are made. Mature Christians are to encourage, yes, but more so by their teaching and life examples to young ones in the faith, as actions speak loudly (sometimes louder than mere words). Then instructing them in basic foundational Truths. Such as *"Forgiveness of sins"* 1 John 1:9,

"If we confess our sins, HE is faithful and just to forgive us our sins and to cleanse us from all unrighteousness."

Following confession, we are completely 'restored' forgiven and being seen as "righteous" in CHRIST JESUS.

And can continue to go-forth with THE SPIRIT WHO resides within, as your heavenly resource.

And that believers (born-again) are the *"Temple of THE HOLY SPIRIT"* - 1 Corinthians 3:16.

Actually we are the Inner Sanctuary, where the presence of ALMIGHTY GOD dwells! Known as 'The Most Holy Place.'

For your spiritual enrichment read 1 Kings 6:1-13, and 8:6-66. About the Temple and King Solomon's dedication. As we are THE LORD'S Temple. As such we are the 'Inner Sanctuary' the very dwelling place of THE LORD GOD! Young believers need to know and understand, the difficulties they face daily, as the evil one continues with his temptations. The evil one's desire is to separate the believer in CHRIST from that inner resource of THE SPIRIT. Therefore, he continues his attacks via, informing the young ones that this temptation is not sin, but what you are entitled to.

1 Corinthians 10:13, - that,
"No temptation has overtaken you except such as is common to man; but GOD is faithful, WHO will not allow you to be tempted beyond what you are able, but with the temptation will also make a way of escape, that you may be able to bear it."

Victory is possible when we are in an abiding relationship with our LORD. As HE gives the overcoming power and deliverance.
Young believers must be aware of the depths of their 'new birth in CHRIST.' 1 John 5:11-12,

"This is the testimony; that GOD has given us eternal life, and this life is in HIS SON. He who has THE SON has life; he who does not have THE SON of GOD does not have life. These things I have written to you who believe in THE NAME of THE SON of GOD, that you may know that you have eternal life, and that you may continue to believe in THE NAME of THE SON of GOD."

Such 'fellowship in the gospel' produces confidence, in THE HOLY SPIRIT'S ministering. As it is written, Philippians 1:6,

"Being confident of this very thing, that HE WHO has begun a good work in you will complete it until the Day of JESUS CHRIST."

It is JESUS WHO has merely begun HIS good work in you. He will continue, daily as you "Abide in HIM" on and until HE calls you home to Glory!

The assembly at Philippi was remembered for 'their fellowship in the gospel' - being presented via the apostle Paul. As their part of the fellowship, was in providing on-going prayer, funds and supplies for 'Paul to go forth.' And today those who assist missionaries and proclaimers of the gospel will be held also in remembrance by THE LORD of GLORY!

4

The Good Work Continues in You

Philippians 1:6-8,

"Being confident of this very thing, that HE WHO has begun a good work in you will complete it until the Day of JESUS CHRIST; Just as it is right for me to think this of you all, because I have you in my heart, inasmuch as both my chains and in defense and confirmation of the gospel, you all are partakers with me of grace. For GOD is my witness, how greatly I long for you all with the affection of JESUS CHRIST."

The good work here is in reference to their support in outreaching to others in different places. As they assisted by helping to fund and especially in their on-going prayers for such. This ministry of theirs was to continue, as they continued in CHRIST. Resulting in strengthening their faith in their relationship with THE LORD of GLORY.

Also THE HOLY SPIRIT, continues HIS ministry with new believers and uses others, such as -
Mature Christians who are to reach out, embracing and encouraging young believers with Scriptural Truths. Mentoring the young and suggesting a place for them to worship. Where they can hear THE WORD, and be taught the Truths.

But even just attending a good gospel preaching assembly is not enough, no!

The young believers are to 'reach up' seek out the spiritual mature ones for their assistance. This is exercising your faith, the first step. In so doing you will become an 'on-going' Christian.

The Old Testament Tabernacle can be used as an illustration.

There, the seeking one was permitted entrance only into the courtyard to offer their sacrifice. At the Altar of Burnt Offering.

Unfortunately today, that is as far as many (if not most) new believers go. Once receiving GOD'S gracious gift of eternal salvation in CHRIST JESUS, via the Cross at Calvary, they merely sit back in the awesome knowledge of CHRIST'S washing their sins away. And do not go forth, gaining fuller spiritual knowledge of THE LORD GOD. And their relationship in and with THE LORD. However, if continuing on, as in reading and studying the Bible, as well seeking assistance from mature Christians. A new believer will understand that they are now – 'a holy priest and a royal priest' (1 Peter 2:5 and 9). Then as such, we are to offer up "Spiritual sacrifices" and then to "Shew forth the praises of HIM WHO hath called you out of darkness into HIS marvelous LIGHT." Thus able to enter into a fuller, deeper relationship with their LORD.
Having the Old Testament Tabernacle as a pattern, we are to venture forth beyond the Altar of Sacrifice to the Bronze Basin for cleansing.

In preparation to enter the Holy Place. The Old Testament priest had to be washed, and cleansed at the Bronze Basin (therein) before he could proceed any further, into the Tabernacle to worship of GOD.

We are to be washed, spiritual cleansing via the water of GOD'S WORD, Ephesians 5:26. Being so cleansed in GOD'S WORD, we may freely enter into the Holy Place. Worshipping there, offering prayers and praise before the Altar of Incense.

Then into the Most Holy Place, as a royal priest into the very presence of THE LORD – "In CHRIST."

Remember in the Old Testament, only the high priest was to enter and that only once a year.

Now as a born-again Christian, you are permitted as a royal priest to enter into the Most Holy Place as often as you desire.

Further, being such, you have now actually, '<u>become</u>' <u>the Most Holy Place</u> as THE SPIRIT OF GOD now dwells within you! Yes, as the TRINITY is in THE SPIRIT dwelling within you, John 14:23.

Therefore, each of us should daily be seeking to be fully prepared (complete) looking forward to the Day of CHRIST! The Day of CHRIST speaks clearly about HIS second coming – as revealed in Revelation 19:11-21

However, born-again Christians will be 'Raptured' up into the Glories of Heavenly Paradise, before that Day! In fact, they will be part of the armies of heaven clothed in white, following THE LORD as HE 'Returns to earth' on 'that Day', Revelation 19:14.

The hearts of all mankind are but an open book to THE LORD. HE not only knows all, but – 2 Chronicles 16:9,- *"For the eyes of THE LORD run to and fro throughout the whole earth, to show HIMSELF strong on behalf of those whose heart is loyal to HIM."*

And the apostle Paul is an excellent example to and for us as we go forth. As he was bound in chains. He mention the chains again in verses 13, 14, and 16. But the chains were not able to hamper nor limit his on-going participation of presenting the gospel. He was not over bound with them, rather he declared that the chains were of CHRIST.

Therefore, the whole palace guard were witness to Paul's constant participation.

He states, how he longs for them. And his prayer includes, -

5

Love Deepened via Application

Philippians 1:9-11,

"And this I pray, that your love may abound still more and more in knowledge and in all discernment, that you may approve the things that are excellent, that you may be sincere and without offense till the Day of CHRIST, being filled with the fruits of righteousness which are by JESUS CHRIST, to the glory and praise of GOD."

And may such prayer be ours. That our –
Love would abound more and more, reaching out to the lost who are bound in the pit of dark disbelief.

Ever increasing in knowledge and discernment, of GOD'S HOLY WORD and its application in and through our daily lives. The phrase, "All discernment" means we are not only to observe the outward, as in having knowledge, but go beyond, seeking the inner depth, making a distinction – not only with words, but life action on our part.

That we approve things that are excellent, assisting others in their belief and, 'out-reach to the un-reached.'

That we may be sincere, reflected in our love, as we seek continuing united participation of the gospel.

And without offense till, -

"The Day of CHRIST,"

The assembly at Philippi was well grounded in the TRUTH of the Holy Scriptures. As THE HOLY SPIRIT did not need to fully explain the, 'Coming of CHRIST in the air and Rapture the born-again believers into Glory for all eternity.'

Read in your Bible, 2 Thessalonians 2:1-3. Here is a portion by Wuest (Prof of Greek at Moody Institute), verse 2:3, -

"... That Day shall not come except the aforementioned departure [of the church to Heaven] comes first ..."

Read in 1 Corinthians 15:51-58, again the Rapture is explained, here is verse 52, -

"In a moment, in the twinkling of an eye, at the last trumpet. For the trumpet will sound, and the dead will be raised incorruptible, and we shall be changed."

Until then we are to be -
"Filled with the Fruits of Righteousness"

Verse 11 states, "Being filled with the fruits of righteousness 'Which are by,' JESUS CHRIST, to the glory and praise of GOD."

That others see CHRIST-likeness in us. Being filled with fruits of righteousness, which are available only in an on-going fellowship with JESUS CHRIST, our SAVIOR, our LORD, that ALMIGHTY GOD be praised!

Being 'filled with fruits of righteousness' is fully explained in John 15:1-8. We are to be as a 'Branch of the TRUE VINE JESUS CHRIST.' That HIS Life may flow into us, as we abide as one of HIS branches. (Obedient branch)

May that be our prayer, not only for ourselves, but for other Christians? And not limited to just our assembly. But 'united' in heart out-cry prayer for union together of all assemblies. Then to go-forth as 'CHRIST'S Ambassadors,' reaching out to the masses in the pit of dark disbelief. Love is much more than a mere word. Love is expression, love is demonstrated and proven through acts!
A man seeking a special woman to be his wedded wife, must show, demonstrate and provide proof. Not just with words, but through his life – such as described in Ephesians 5:25, -

"Husbands love your wives, just as CHRIST also loved the church and gave HIMSELF for her."

A man seeking a special woman, must provide proof of who he is. As his desire is for her to set her life aside – and join together with him. Then to do this, the man is instructed to show his love as CHRIST did in loving the church!

JESUS CHRIST set HIS Life, HIS Heavenly Throne in Glory aside – in obedience to ALMIGHTY GOD THE FATHER. CHRIST set all aside, "In Love for fallen mankind" providing the Only Way to escape the pit of condemnation because of Adam's disobedience.

There is another kind of separating deep love and commitment, 2 Timothy 2:3,

"... Endure hardship as a good soldier of JESUS CHRIST. No one engaged in warfare entangles himself with the affairs of this life, that he may please HIM WHO enlisted him as a soldier."

A soldier is one who so loves his country, that he is willing to set his life and desires aside. Soldiers surrender their lives (and many give them) over to their country when they are so called.

This is the 'abounding love' that THE SPIRIT is making known to us – that we should express such with our lives, that is demonstrating as we go forth with our LORD! Philippians 1:9 begins with, *"And this I pray."*

THE SPIRIT, is using the life of Paul as an example to and for us. That we Christians will experience having a loving prayer life of outreach.

And this I pray, that your love ... This is addressed to, "All the saints in CHRIST."

A saint that is "In CHRIST" experiencing prayer with abounding love, will know no bounds in his/her outreach.

I personally know of such a saint "In CHRIST."
This individual, was drafted into the U.S. Army and stationed in Germany. One night THE LORD revealed to him in a dream, the death of a friend of his. The dream was extremely vivid, showing his friend who was driving his utility truck through a heavy rain storm.

Suddenly the road being covered in deep mud, a drunk driver coming the opposite direction, lost control in the mud and crashed into him head-on. The drunk was going 70 miles per hour, his friend 50. The left front wheel of the truck was driven back under the dash. The truck was violently thrown to the right. The driver's door opened and he was thrown out and crushed between the car and the truck. The dream ended with the truck off the road to the right, the car turned back in the direction it came. And his friend's dead body was lying in the mud.

The saint (soldier) saw it all in a dream, therefore he, in prayer of love abounding, leaped out of bed and seeking assurance from THE LORD of GLORY that HE, THE LORD would not permit this to happen to his friend.

His friend's accident occurred the next day just exactly as he was shown in his dream.

Less than two weeks later the soldier's father passed away into Heaven's Glory. And he was home on emergency leave. And most all of the fellow utility workers who knew the soldier were there to express their condolences.

One crossed the room and in a loud voice called out to the driver of the truck, "How is it that you are not dead?" I saw your truck today and it is completely demolished.

And it is not possible that anyone could survive that crash. You should at least be in the hospital with all kinds of life threating injuries!"

The soldier said to his driver friend, let's go in the hall and talk. There the soldier told in 'exact detail' the entire accident scene. His driver friend was shocked, "Who could have possibly told you all those details as there was no witnesses and I have not told anyone?"

The soldier said, "I had a dream, and the dream showed every detail, with one exception!" What was the exception? He said, "You were killed and your body was lying in the mud."

But I got out of bed and prayed and prayed, telling THE LORD that I would not answer the Reveille Call and would not stop praying until YOU, my LORD assure me that this will not happen! THE LORD answered him, saying, "It will not happen."

The truck friend said, "Do you know that, at the moment of impact and my truck was violently thrown to the right, I was being thrown out of the truck, but the door came slamming against me. I was forced to go to the doctors, and all he could find wrong was a bruise on my left hip the size of a 25 cent piece, as the door pushed me back into the truck!?"

The drunk driver and his passenger were both taken to the hospital. As the passenger in the car was thrown through the windshield, his face a bloody mess. The passenger was a hitch hiker and he explained of their stopping in town for a few drinks and beers and then going 70 (in heavy rain) at the time of the crash!

Philippians 1:10-11, "... *you be sincere and without offense till the Day of CHRIST, being filled with the fruits of righteousness which are by JESUS CHRIST, to the glory and praise of GOD."*

Yes, answers to such prayers as the soldier/saint in Germany are only possible by in and through JESUS CHRIST!

As he was in (and continues) in an abiding union, as a branch of CHRIST. John 15:7-8, -

"If you abide in ME, and MY WORDS abide in you, you will ask what you desire, and it shall be done for you. By this MY FATHER is glorified, that you bear much fruit; so you will be MY disciples."

And there is another Scripture that is an example. 2 Samuel 19:31-39, here is just a few portions. –

'Now Barzillai, had provided King David with supplies while he was in exile across the Jordan River (Mahanaim). King David requested Barzillai to return to Jerusalem with him, and he would provide for him there. Barzillai replied that he would like to stay and be buried near his father's grave.

The king answered, 'Now, whatever you request of me, I will do for you.'

Whatever you request of me, I will do for you.

When you and I are in an abiding relationship with our LORD, seeking further knowledge of HIM and HIS WORD. Abounding in HIS love, then we also will be filled with fruits of righteousness. As we serve, not only an earthly king, but …

"THE KING of KINGS and LORD of LORDS"

As the Scripture declared, *"Ask what you desire, and it shall be done for you."*

"If you abide in ME, and MY WORDS abide in you, you will ask what you desire, and it shall be done for you. By this MY FATHER is glorified, that you bear much fruit; so you will be MY disciples." John 15:7-8

6

Things which Happen

Philippians 1:12-14, -

"But I want you to know, brethren, that the things which happened to me have actually turned out for the furtherance of the gospel, so that it has become evident to the whole palace guard, and to all the rest, that my chains are in CHRIST; and most of the brethren in THE LORD, having become confident by my chains are much more bold to speak the WORD without fear.

The apostle Paul was a giant of faith and belief in JESUS CHRIST! He does not complain nor is he embittered with the chains that hold and restrict him.

Just the opposite is his reaction. *"The things which happened to me have actually turned out for the furtherance of the gospel."* All mature Christians are to come to the place of realization that whatever happens –

> 'Is not by chance, nor a coincidence'
> Of circumstances.

Rather, things that happen to a saint, are the direct result of and according to ALMIGHTY GOD'S Plan and HIS Purposes. Or via HIS permissive will, again for HIS Plans and Purposes.

Wuest's Word Studies of the phrase, -

"Furtherance of the gospel."

The Greek meaning for the word, furtherance is, = 'To cut before' – that is to remove and prepare a way that was not possible before.

This was such a reference to the fast moving Greek Army as they took control of the entire empire in a mere eight (8) years! But an army that is holding large shields (2 by 4 feet) and long spears is encumbered and slowed down (if not stopped) by heavy over growth and dense woods. Therefore, an army of specialists went ahead clearing a wide path, removing the overgrown brush and clusters of heavy young trees. So the rapidly advancing army could go quickly, straight through. Not having to detour many miles or days around the obstacle of overgrowth.
As such, we born-again Christians are to be as a special movement preparing the way for THE LORD to enter the hearts of others! Our lives removing any doubt to and for the yet, unbelievers. Leaving a broad opening for the gospel of good news of JESUS CHRIST!

The Jews were against the gospel, (read in Acts 21:26-on) and had an uproar (riot) against Paul for being a proclaimer of CHRIST. Roman soldiers intervene rescuing Paul, but placed him in chains.

As you know Paul is taken to Rome and held a prisoner and guarded by soldiers for years. Now the special guard unit of the Emperor, known as the 'Praetorium Guard' (KJV and the NKJV, state the palace guard). Were certainly not open to the gospel of JESUS CHRIST.

Therefore, for the – 'Furtherance' of the gospel of Good News, Paul is placed in chains and held progressively by the Praetorium guards who were rotated daily. Therefore, most 'all of this special unit' were witnessed to by Paul. Also Paul had many Christian visitors, who together with Paul conversed almost daily about JESUS CHRIST. Thus the Scripture states in 1:13, -

"It has become evident to the whole Praetorium guard, and to all the rest, that my chains are in CHRIST."

Resulting in all the guard unit and 'all the rest' having heard the gospel of JESUS CHRIST!

Yes, all the rest, including up and into the Emperors entire household! Have heard the Good News about JESUS CHRIST as SAVIOR and LORD!

Thus, Paul's chains were a 'Happening for the 'furtherance' of the gospel.

Question, what is 'said and remembered' about the 'things which happened' to you and I?

How have are our reactions been seen and understood? As an obstacle or as a, 'clearing'? Thus opening the way for others to progress into a deeper and fuller relationship with THE LORD of GLORY!

Philippians 1:14, -

"And most of the brethren in THE LORD, having become confident by my chains are much more bold to speak the WORD without fear.

At first reading this verse is difficult. Mainly because Paul says, -

"Become confident by my chains, are much more bold to speak the WORD."

Confident because of Paul's chains? Does that mean, they were glad? Or confident because Paul was out of the way in prison? Or is it as they now speak, they do not have to be concerned of his overriding their statements, correcting them?

Let's keep verse 14 in context with verses 12 and 13.

There, they observe that Paul is not upset, he is not complaining, rather he is rejoicing that his chains, are 'of CHRIST.' It is not only known, but has become, -

"Evident to the whole Praetorium guard, and to all the rest, that my chains are in CHRIST."

There were Christians in Rome, but were they 'out-going'? Or because of the political climate they were not bold in presenting the Good News?

Verse 14 starts out with, -

"Most of the brethren in THE LORD."

Paul refers to them as, "In THE LORD" that is a good phrase, stating of their relationship in and with CHRIST. Thus, Paul is not degrading them with this phrase, -

---

Do All Things Through Christ

"Confident by my chains are much more bold to speak the WORD without fear."

Just the opposite, believers in CHRIST seeing what has taken place, throughout much of Rome, including up and even into the palace. And Paul is confident, not complaining, rather well pleased in his chains!

Therefore, because of THE HOLY SPIRIT led life of Paul. His abiding in JESUS CHRIST as his SAVIOR and LORD, and not overwhelmed by his circumstances.

The brethren are now, going forth, in spite of the political climate with the good news, being bold as Paul, proclaiming THE WORD without fear!

7

Rejoice in Things that Happen

Philippians 1:15-18, -

"Some indeed preach CHRIST even from envy and strife, and some also from goodwill: the former preach CHRIST from selfish ambition, not sincerely, supposing to add to my chains; but the latter out of love, knowing that I am appointed for the defense of the gospel. What then? Only that in every way, whether in pretense or in truth, CHRIST is preached; and in this I rejoice, yes, and will rejoice."

Prior to this, THE SPIRIT has Paul stating that the things which happened to him worked towards the 'furtherance' of the gospel.

Now he is rejoicing even though he is the subject of strife and those who envy his steadfastness and victory over his chains!

During this time period, there was a group against Paul's, HOLY SPIRIT led teaching of the gospel of CHRIST. This group (Judaizers) were stating, that all coming to CHRIST had to come first via the way of the Jewish Law.

Requiring the Gentiles to first be adherents to the Jewish Law. Then be centered in CHRIST. So they were happy that the apostle Paul was locked up and could not come forth to counter their un-Scriptural teachings.

However, there was a much larger group, continuing to present the Truths of Christianity. Fully knowing that none were ever able to keep the law. As the law was to show them where they were in relation to ALMIGHTY GOD and HIS Truths.

The Old Testament teaches us, that 'Blessings came as the result of obedience,' to ALMIGHTY GOD, HIS commands, judgments, precepts and ordinances.

And disobedience resulted in terrible consequences. Whereas Grace and TRUTH came by JESUS CHRIST and is abundantly 'poured forth' freely onto those who truly believe!

John 1:16-17, *"And of HIS fullness have all we received, and grace for grace. For the law was given by Moses, but grace and TRUTH came by JESUS CHRIST."*

And were anxious and excited to be part of the outreach, presenting the gospel Truths of JESUS CHRIST as SAVIOR and LORD!

Unfortunately today we have various groups, setting forth, 'adding' their, shall we say, 'traditional views' and not adhering strictly to Scriptural Truths. Therein continuing disunity and confusing those who are in unbelief.

Therefore, resulting in our once great country, being in the foul state that we now are experiencing. The liberal 'left leaning judges' supporting the out cries of the atheists demands, that the Bible and crosses be removed and not permitted on any public property. Demanding that, "In GOD we Trust" be removed from our currency. Also that the "Commandments" of GOD be removed from our Court Houses.

Today, Bibles have been (past tense) removed from Veterans centers. Military chaplains are not permitted to proclaim JESUS CHRIST and eternal salvation through HIM! Some high ranking officers have been removed, because they voiced belief in JESUS CHRIST!

And of course Bibles and prayer have also been removed from all public schools.

I do recall a judge in Florida (some years ago) who was petitioned to establish a special day for atheists. Their reason being, that Christians have Christmas and Easter. The judge replied, well you already have your special day set aside for you.

How is that they complained? The judge replied, you atheists are fools as you do not believe in GOD!

Therefore, April 1st fool's day is your special day set apart for you.

8

CHRIST magnified in you

Philippians 1:19-21, -

"For I know that this will turn out for my deliverance through your prayer and supply of THE SPIRIT of JESUS CHRIST, according to my earnest expectation and hope that in nothing I shall be ashamed, but with all boldness, be always, so now also CHRIST will be magnified in my body, whether by life or by death. For me to live is CHRIST, and to die is gain."

This portion is also a bit difficult to readily grasp at first. As the old KJV states, -

"This shall turn to my salvation through your prayer."

Here in the NKJV states, -

"This will turn out for my deliverance through your prayer and the supply of THE SPIRIT of CHRIST."

Also a number of translations, state, 'Salvation instead of deliverance.'

Wuest's Greek professor at Moody, (expanded) translation puts it forth as this, -

"For I know that this [the fact that CHRIST is being proclaimed] shall result in deliverance and preservation for me [lest I become discouraged in and because of my imprisonment which restricts my opportunity to proclaim the good news] through your petition and through the full-proportioned support and aid of THE SPIRIT of JESUS CHRIST. And this is exactly in accordance with my undivided and intense expectancy and hope, namely, that with respect to not even one thing shall I be put to shame [defeated], but in every boldness, courage, and fearlessness of uninhibited freedom of speech as always so also now, CHRIST shall be conspicuously and gloriously manifested in my body, whether through [a continued] life [on earth] or through [a martyrs'] death, for, so far as I am concerned, to be living, both as to my very existence and my experience, [that is] CHRIST, and to have died, that would be a gain."
End quote from Wuest's translation. Capital letters for or about CHRIST is of HR.

Wuest's translation puts it clearly, that the man Paul, would be 'delivered' from discouragement, because the gospel proclamation is not being halted, through his prison bonds.

Further, that Paul would be encouraged through the prayers of the faithful in CHRIST. Especially by the full-proportioned support and aid of THE SPIRIT of JESUS CHRIST.

Christians are not overlords, no. Christians are to be loyal, faithful and obedient servants to their heavenly MASTER. The key is –
        "Obedience to THE WORD of GOD."

As therein, THE SPIRIT ministers to the faithful, obedient and loyal ones.

Our LORD said, 'A faithful and wise servant, is one whom when his MASTER comes, finds he has been obedient.'

This is the message of THE HOLY SPIRIT to us in this our day. As we are not, nor have we been imprisoned, for our belief, or testifying of the good news. We as, 'individuals' have not been hampered nor even restricted, (yet) here in the U.S.A. –

However, in pretense or in truth, 'CHRIST has, 'Not' been proclaimed, nor is the Good News and Great Truth now being proclaimed here in the once great United States of America, by and through the everyday born-again Christian?!' Why?

What will be our excuse?

Yes, there has been and there now is, some faithful pastor presenters, some evangelists and some writers, but the majority of Christians, in the United States of America have remained silent and continue in silence to our everlasting shame!

And most unfortunately even in their own homes?!? Children 'reflect their parents' and their values.
And the utter lack of Christian basic beliefs are not known nor understood. Instead what is sweeping across our nation, - is riots, setting our cities afire, trashing cars, looting stores and killing police officers – but, BUT the so-called Christian community has remained silent?!?!

What we need is a 'great up-ward outcry' similar to Paul, but 'seeking deliverance' from our discouragement' that has overwhelmed us, because of our lack of being fully supplied (filled) with THE HOLY SPIRIT! And not being loyally, faithfully and Obedient to our LORD'S Commands.

The faithful and loyally obedient servant Paul's expectation was, that, in nothing he was to be ashamed, and with all boldness he wanted CHRIST to be glorified in his body!

Question, what is your expectation? Have you spoken out, let alone in boldness? Is JESUS CHRIST being presented, let alone magnified by your body (life style)? (Sadly I visited a church where the pastor had on un-pressed pants and a pull over for shirt. And of the some 3,000 present at least 500 had on baseball caps. And 500 had on only shorts, undershirts and sneakers.)

Compare the above observation with what THE HOLY SPIRIT, states in Colossians 2:8, -

"Beware unless anyone cheat you through philosophy and empty deceit, according to the tradition of men, according to the basic principles of the world, and not according to CHRIST."

There is 'no excuse' or limitations, yet. But there are many requests, by certain groups to our government to silence Christianity. What we need, we must have an abiding relationship with JESUS CHRIST our SAVIOR and LORD. Therein, be 'filled' (supplied) to go forth (not sitting in shamed defeat) that CHRIST be gloriously manifested in the likes of us.

Remember, Colossians 2:10, -

"… You are complete in HIM (JESUS), WHO is the Head of all principality and power."

May, our 'out-cry' be,

"For to me, to live is CHRIST, and to die is gain."

9

To Live is CHRIST

Philippians 1:21-26, -

"For to me, to live is CHRIST, and to die is gain. But if I live on in the flesh, this will mean fruit from my labor; yet what I shall choose I cannot tell. For I am hard pressed between the two, having a desire to depart and be with CHRIST, which is far better. Nevertheless to remain in the flesh is more needful for you. And being confident of this, I know that I shall remain and continue with you all for your progress and joy of faith, that your rejoicing for me may be more abundant in JESUS CHRIST by my coming to you again."

Yes, the chapter 8 (of this earthly book, by HR) before this 'ended' with, -

"For me to live is CHRIST and to die is gain." And now this chapter (9 of this earthly book) 'begins' with, *"For me to live is CHRIST and to die is gain."*

The reason is outstanding as the life of a born-again Christian – begins with CHRIST and praise ALMIGHTY GOD, the ending of this earthly life is but another awesome beginning – without end as it is eternal!!! With THE LORD JESUS CHRIST in the Glories of Heaven!!!

Therefore, may we shout out together, –

"For me to live is CHRIST and to die is gain."

There are so many Scriptures that declare, of JESUS CHRIST giving life, here are but a very few.

John 1:12, *"But as many as received HIM (CHRIST), to them HE gave the right to become children of GOD, to those who believe in HIS NAME."*

John 5:21, *"For as THE FATHER raises the dead and gives life to them, even so THE SON gives life to whom HE will."*

And there are numerous Scriptures, revealing of a heavenly life to those who "Believe in JESUS CHRIST." John 3:16, *"For GOD so loved the world that HE gave HIS only begotten SON, that whoever believes in HIM should not perish but have everlasting life."*

THE LORD JESUS CHRIST speaking in John 5:24, - *"Most assuredly, I say unto you, he who hears MY WORD and believes in HIM WHO sent ME has everlasting life, and shall not come into judgment, but has passed from death into life."*

And one of the most important, WORDS of declaration is from JESUS CHRIST HIMSELF, in John 14:6, -

*"**I AM the Way, the Truth, and the Life**. No one comes to THE FATHER except through ME."*

The people of the world, exist. They have breath and growth and even some obtain old age. They exist for and about themselves. Some acquire wives to have children, but these women are referred to as merely their possessions and not partners of a life, of togetherness as, 2 = 1.

Others all across this earthly world are engaged in wars and rumors of wars. Because each are seeking and reaching out only for their own desires. How sad, and some even think that slaying others is a benefit to them?! That describes the lives of the people of the world. Why? Because they are born, under ALMIGHTY GOD'S Condemnation! The result of Adam's sin in the beginning of not obeying GOD'S WORD! This is clearly set forth in John 3:17-18, -

"For GOD did not send HIS SON into to the world to condemn the world, but that the world through HIM might be saved. He who believes in HIM is not condemned; but he who does not believe is condemned already, because he has not believed in THE NAME of the only BEGOTTEN SON of GOD."

The entire world is under ALMIGHTY GOD'S Condemnation. The peoples therein merely exist, without any hope. Then following this life under condemnation, they are released into, the eternal lake of GOD'S Wrathful Judgment Hell fire!

Unless, unless they turn to THE LORD JESUS CHRIST. This is the message from THE HOLY SPIRIT to those who will hear and turn to CHRIST. By faith believing, becoming born-again Christian believers.

Thus the Philippian message is to –
"All the saints In CHRIST"

It is not limited to the Plymouth Brethren, as they are special saints, yes. So are the Methodists special, the Independents, Mennonites, Presbyterians, Baptists, and the list continues on –

"All the saints In CHRIST!" You are not special belonging to a certain denomination, no! You are special to the hosts of heaven, those who believe in CHRIST and having received the precious gift of eternal life!

Wearing a cross or going to a church once in a while does not make you a Christian.

As a youth, I thought I was a Christian, because I knew that I was not born to Jewish parents.

THE HOLY SPIRIT has inspired this portion of Scripture to 'stir us up' –

As we act as if we are bond by chains of certain limitations! THE SPIRIT has shouted, that even iron chains do not matter, then what is holding us back?

Merely the chains of our lack of 'faith' and being bound merely by the shackles of our faithless imagination!

10

Worthy of the Gospel

Philippians 1:27-30, -

"Only let your conduct be worthy of the gospel of CHRIST, so that whether I come and see you or am absent, I may hear of your affairs, that you stand fast in in one spirit, with one mind striving together for the faith of the gospel, and not in any way terrified by your adversaries, which to them is a proof of perdition, but to you of salvation, and that from GOD. For to you it has been granted on behalf of CHRIST, not only to believe in HIM, but also to suffer for HIS sake, having the same conflict which you saw in me and now hear in me."

Remember THE HOLY SPIRIT is the Author and the great apostle Paul is no longer with us. But this portion of Scripture is directed to - "All the saints in CHRIST JESUS" (1:1).

Therefore, THE ONE WHO desires "to see" and "hear of our (life) affairs" is THE SPIRIT of GOD.

Mankind has a self-centered esteem of having, great worth. As all think that they are worthy of a higher position, worthy of being more highly recognized, worthy of a great spouse, and so on.

But, has the affairs of our lives revealed, that we, saints of our LORD, are worthy of the gospel of JESUS CHRIST? Oswald Chambers speaks of this in his daily devotional. He states, 'There is nothing easier than getting into a right relationship with GOD except when it is not GOD WHOM you want but only what HE gives.' Portions from April 27th.

John 16:32, JESUS CHRIST speaking to HIS disciples shortly before HIS being betrayed by Judas states, *"Indeed the hour is coming, yes, has now come, that you will be scattered, each to his own, and will leave ME alone."*

Oswald Chambers addresses this – 'Are we prepared for this? It is not that we choose it, but GOD engineers our circumstances so that we are brought there. Until we have been brought through that experience, our faith is bolstered up by feelings and by blessings. When once we get there, no matter where GOD places us or what the inner desolations are, we can praise GOD that all is well. That is faith being worked out in actualities.' End of partial quote of April 4th.

Philippians 1:27 expounds, lays open that our conduct (conversation) is to be in worthiness of the gospel of JESUS CHRIST. Such to be revealed by our –

Standing fast in one spirit
Standing fast in one mind
Striving together for the faith of the gospel

'Standing Fast' is an old military term. As such it is used some four times in Ephesians 6:11-14. Soldiers of JESUS CHRIST are to "Stand" against the wiles of the devil. Be armored with all GOD'S armor that we may "Withstand" in the evil day, and having done all, to "Stand." "Stand" therefore being girded with truth, having on the breastplate of righteousness ...

Doing so together in the spirit of togetherness and with one mind, 'united.' Provides an open and clear message to the lost peoples of our once great nation!

Striving is not to be misunderstood, here is the meaning = 'association, companionship, wrestle in company with, to seek jointly, labour with, together for.'

Our mind-set is to be, reaching the goal that is before us, being victorious like a football team, striving together. Being so united, we can 'stand fast', holding the Fort of Truthfulness of the gospel of CHRIST!

Philippians 1:28, -

"And not in any way terrified by your adversaries, which is to them proof of 'perdition."

Perdition = utter loss of soul, entire loss; ruin, damnation. Those who are against Christianity and Christians are in this lost sate of damnation! And their actions of hate and disagreement provide you with proof of your salvation in CHRIST! Therein rejoice and not be terrified of them.

For HE WHO is on your side is far greater, than the entire company of the unbelievers.

As Christians are endowed with a 'Special Force' much like the elite in the military, but even far Greater and even more Powerful!

The following is but a 'small sample portion' of these Special Forces, who operate without being seen or known! Psalm 34:1-10, -

"I will bless THE LORD at all times; HIS praise shall be continually in my mouth. My soul shall make its boast in THE LORD; the humble shall hear of it and be glad. Oh, magnify THE LORD with me, and let us exalt HIS NAME together. I sought THE LORD, and HE heard me, and delivered me from all my fears. They looked to HIM and were radiant, and their faces were not ashamed. This poor man cried out, and THE LORD him, and saved out of all his troubles.

(Psalm 34:7), **The Angel of THE LORD encamps all around those who fear HIM, and delivers them.**

Oh, taste and see that THE LORD is good; blessed is the man who trusts in HIM! Oh, fear THE LORD, you HIS saints! There is no want to those who fear HIM. The young lions lack and suffer hunger; but those who seek THE LORD shall not lack any good thing."

What promises from ALMIGHTY GOD WHO - keeps HIS WORD! I have set verse 34:7 apart, trusting that you will memorize it and remind yourself, when others or circumstances seem to surround you. That far greater is the 'angel of THE LORD who surrounds' you to deliver you!

And Psalm 34 continues, with verse 15, *"The eyes of THE LORD are on the righteous. And HIS ears are open to their cry."*

Verse 17, *"The righteous cry out, and THE LORD hears, and delivers them out of all their troubles."*

Verse 22, *"THE LORD redeems the soul of HIS servants, and none of those who trust in HIM shall be condemned."*

Psalm 35 continues the angel's arms of embracement around you.

Verses 5 and 6 is to those who are against you, seeking your harm.
"… Let the angel of THE LORD chase them. Let their way be dark and slippery, and let the angel of THE LORD pursue them."

2 Chronicles 16:9, -

"For the eyes of THE LORD run to and fro throughout the whole earth, to show HIMSELF strong on behalf of those heart is loyal to HIM."

Therefore, we are not to be concerned, let alone terrified of, 'any adversary.'

But please note* to whom the angel of THE LORD delivers. Is to those who *"fear HIM"* this fear is not being terrified, no. this is reverential trust, belief and worship. The Hebrew word for 'fear' of THE LORD means = reverence.

And Psalm 5:12, states it to those who, –

"For YOU O LORD, will bless the righteous; with favor YOU will surround him as with a shield."

Therefore, seek and assure yourself of your relationship, your abiding in JESUS CHRIST. And JESUS CHRIST'S WORDS are abiding in you. John 15:1-8. And that 'all' your sins are confessed.

THE HOLY SPIRIT has added, if, if we are called to suffer on behalf of CHRIST, remain steadfast in your belief and look forward to HIS awesome hand of deliverance.

11

Esteem Others Better

Philippians 2:1-4, -

"Therefore if there is any consolation in CHRIST, if any comfort of love, if any fellowship of THE SPIRIT, if any affection and mercy, fulfill my joy by being like-minded, having the same love, being of one accord, of one mind. Let nothing be done through selfish ambition or conceit, but in lowliness of mind let each esteem others better than himself. Let each of you look out not only for his own interests, but also for the interests of others."

If we are, "In CHRIST" we are also in a state of consolation. That is we have been consoled, comforted and set apart as HIS very OWN, for HIS Plans and HIS Purposes. By and through JESUS CHRIST HIMSELF! Resting assured in HIS everlasting embrace, we are to be in fellowship, together, united, and enjoined by the very presence of THE SPIRIT of GOD in each of us!

And in verse 2 we are exhorted by THE SPIRIT (WHO is the Author) to bring joy to HIM via our obedience, being in one, like-minded sentiment. Referring to THE SPIRIT, yes, as Paul the servant is no longer with us. But THE SPIRIT has never left us. And 'All Scriptures' are to and for all Christians everywhere, throughout the world.

We are not to study, nor limit the Holy Scriptures merely as historical and relating to those early first days only. Oh, no!

We are to apply them to our Christian beliefs, and lives, learning and being obedient therein, today and every day. I am aware of some men, desiring to become pastors. However, first and foremost is this question, 'have they been called' by THE LORD JESUS CHRIST to so do? And I am also fully aware of some parents seeking and desiring such for their sons.

We are not to seek such. Thinking that we are able and have the ambition to so do. No!

Just the opposite, we are first, to consider ourselves in lowliness. Esteeming all others better than ourselves. Therein, that state of mind, following and being obedient to ALMIGHTY GOD'S WORD, THE LORD may use you in HIS plans in such a capacity. But first, one must apply Scriptures to his life and set self aside, that GOD may do the selection. This is not easy for the natural man.

 Born-again Christians are no longer natural, but spiritual, seeking and desiring that ALMIGHTY GOD may have HIS way in and with us for HIS Glory.

Setting self aside - (this is, taking up your cross and to follow JESUS) is the first essential part of the spiritual growth, being obedient to GOD'S HOLY WORD! If we are unable to accomplish this, then how can we expect to be used as spiritual teachers and leaders? Fully realizing that in a teaching or leading capacity, means being a servant of

CHRIST. And in this service, to 'all others,' as in under and not over.

Our LORD says to HIS believers, in Luke 9:23, -

"And HE said to them all, if any man will come after ME, let him deny himself, and take up his cross daily and follow ME."

This means we are to set our desires, wants and wishes aside. Take the cross, realizing that you are to be crucified with CHRIST! That is setting self aside that THE LORD of GLORY may minister in and through you for HIS Plans and HIS Purposes!

This is best when you 'Apply' John 15:1-8 to your life. JESUS CHRIST describes HIMSELF as THE TRUE VINE. And THE FATHER as the DRESSER of the Vineyard. You, the faith believing, is to see yourself as one of THE TRUE VINES branches! Seeking to be abiding obediently as a branch, bearing HIS Fruit. And a branch that is bowing down laden heavy with fruit, is 'Supported, cared for and looked after by THE VINE DRESSER!'

Therein, being one of THE LORD'S branches, HE may seek through you as –

Looking after the young Christians in your assembly? Do you know who is having spiritual difficulties? As well those having difficulties making ends meet? Do you know who has been missing lately?

Another question is – do you even care? Or are you satisfied to just attend and go home as quickly as possible? This is what 2:4 is about, -

THE HOLY SPRIT is using the life of Paul as an example to and for us. Paul was in chains, having lost his freedom for some years now, but, but he was deeply concerned for the welfare of the Christian believers back in Philippi.
"Let each of you look out not only for his own interests, but also for the interests of others."

This is what the saints are to be about. In 1:27 we read, -

"Only let your conduct be worthy of the gospel of CHRIST ..."
Seeking the well-being of others 'first.'

12

A servant's mind

Philippians 2:5-7, -

"Let this mind be in you which was also in CHRIST JESUS, WHO, being in the form of GOD, did not consider it robbery to be equal with GOD, but made HIMSELF no reputation, taking the form of a bond-servant, and coming in the likeness of men."

We need to keep Scripture in context, not lift a verse out and suggest that it means such and such. And that is the case here in 2:5. As 2:5 is a continuing of verses 2:2-4.

'The mind that is one, having the same love, being of one accord, and not self-seeking. The mindset that will bring joy to the GOD HEAD. Then in humbleness reach out to all others, esteeming them better than yourself!

This is the mind of CHRIST that we are to exhibit to the 'lost souls' of this world.

This is the message of THE SPIRIT, to *"All saints in CHRIST JESUS."* This is, *"HE WHO has begun a good work in you will complete it until the Day of CHRIST."* This is part of, *"Being filled with the fruits of righteousness which are by JESUS CHRIST, to the glory and praise of GOD."* This is CHRIST being magnified in our bodies.

"Let this mind be in you which was also in   CHRIST JESUS."

THE LORD JESUS CHRIST, THE CREATOR of the entire universe and THE SUSTAINER of all things, left HIS Throne in the Glories of Heaven and became in the likeness of one of HIS earthly creations – man. And not only as a mere man, but a bond-servant of men?!!? Therefore,

> *"Let this mind be in you which was also in CHRIST JESUS."*

Ephesians 1:22-23, -

"And HE put all things under HIS feet, and gave HIM to be head over all things to the church, which is HIS body, the fullness of HIM WHO fills all in all."

And yes, we are to have the mind of CHRIST as, <u>we are HIS body</u>! We are HIS arms reaching out to the lost of this world. We are HIS hands to hold and embrace the needy. We are HIS feet to go forth with the message of the Good News. We are his voice to speak, declaring HIS Truths, as CHRIST is the only Way, CHRIST is the Truth and CHRIST is The Life.

May we go, following in obedience, 'Like Minded' as our LORD'S bond-servants?

13

JESUS CHRIST is LORD

Philippians 2:8-11, -

"And being found in appearance as a man, HE humbled HIMSELF and became obedient to the point of death, even the death of the cross. Therefore GOD also has highly exalted HIM and given HIM THE NAME which is above every name, that at THE NAME of JESUS every knee should bow, of those in heaven, and of those on earth, and of those under the earth, and that every tongue should confess that JESUS CHRIST is LORD, to the glory of GOD THE FATHER."

The entire WORD of GOD is revealing Truths to us about our SAVIOR, our LORD JESUS CHRIST and WHO HE is! John 1:1-4, -

"In the beginning was THE WORD, and THE WORD was with GOD, and THE WORD was GOD. HE was in the beginning with GOD. All things were made through HIM, and without HIM nothing was made that was made. In HIM was LIFE, and THE LIFE was THE LIGHT of men."

JESUS CHRIST is THE WORD, and JESUS CHRIST is our life – if (if) we believe, and receive HIS Gracious GIFT, of eternal life, via the forgiveness of our sins, being washed in HIS Blood at the Cross at Calvary.

You, and all mankind were created for one purpose, and that purpose was/is for HIS Creations to honor and glorify their CREATOR! Isaiah 43:7

JESUS CHRIST, THE CREATOR and SUSTAINER of all things, left HIS Throne in Glory becoming as a man. Was obedient to ALMIGHTY GOD THE FATHER, including giving HIS life as a sacrifice, a ransom paying the price (sacrificial death) for our sins – past, present and future! Present and future, yes! If (if) we confess our sins. As our LORD has provided for us in 1 John 1:7-9, -

"But if we walk in the light as HE is THE LIGHT, we have fellowship with one another, and the Blood of JESUS CHRIST HIS SON cleanses us from all sin. If we say that we have no sin, we deceive ourselves, and the Truth is not in us.

Verse 9, **If we confess our sins, HE is faithful and just to forgive us our sins and to cleanse us from all unrighteousness."**

We are to confess, in sorrow of our failure (sin) and be returned, restored via repentance.

Repentance means = to change one's mind with regard to the past or intended action or conduct.

Change the direction of your life, your heart, mind and spirit anew, seeking a higher embracement with THE LORD!

That is we are to be sorry for our disobedience, confess the sin and turn around taking a direction of obedience to ALMIGHTY GOD through HIS WORD!

***The most important point is, it is not according to our ability to walk in traditions, keeping certain rituals nor reciting creeds, and not holding to doctrines or limited beliefs, no!

It is 'All about our keeping, and maintaining a relationship, a fellowship, an abiding union in JESUS CHRIST as our SAVIOR and LORD! As our LORD is THE HEAD!

Here is Oswald Chamber's "My Utmost for HIS HIGHEST" daily devotional for April 6th.
Quote –

'WHO HIS OWN SELF bare our sins in HIS OWN Body on the tree.' 1 Peter 2:24,

'The Cross of JESUS is the revelation of GOD'S judgment on sin. Never tolerate the idea of martyrdom about the Cross of JESUS CHRIST. The Cross was a superb triumph in which the foundations of hell were shaken. There is nothing more certain in time or eternity than that which JESUS CHRIST did on the Cross: HE switched the whole of the human race back into a right relationship with GOD. HE made Redemption the basis of human life, that is, HE made a way for every son of man to get into communion (re-united in fellowship) with GOD.

The Cross did not happen to JESUS: HE came on purpose for it. HE is "THE LAMB slain from the foundation of the world." The whole meaning of the Incarnation is the Cross. Beware of separating GOD manifest in the flesh from THE SON becoming sin. The Incarnation was for the purpose of Redemption. GOD became incarnate for the purpose of putting away sin; not for the purpose of Self-realization. The Cross is the center of Time and of Eternity, the answer to the enigmas of both.

The Cross is not the cross of man but the Cross of GOD, and the Cross of GOD can never be realized in human experience. The Cross is the exhibition of the nature of GOD, the gateway whereby any individual of the human race can enter into union with GOD. When we get to the Cross, we do not go through it; we abide in the life to which the Cross is the gateway, (open to those who believe).

The center of salvation is the Cross of JESUS, and the reason it is so easy to obtain salvation is because it cost GOD so much. The Cross is the point where GOD and sinful man merge with a crash and the way to life is opened – but the crash is on the heart of GOD.'

End quote from Oswald Chambers. Capital letters for or about GOD are of HR.

Therein, that loving union, THE HOLY SPIRIT will minister to, and in and for us – that, HE may minister through us!

In such a union and belief, please know and understand, if THE SPIRIT is able to minister in and through you – then it is 'Not of you.'

Ours is to be in that unified fellowship with our LORD that HE may use our lives, as HIS body for HIS honor and glory!

2:11, *"That every tongue should confess that JESUS CHRIST is our LORD, to the glory of GOD THE FATHER."*

2:10, *"That at THE NAME of JESUS every knee should bow, of those in heaven, and of those on earth, and of those under the earth."*

Please read Revelation chapters 6 through 19 and realize the terrible horror that is 'going to occur' to all disbelievers of ALMIGHTY GOD'S WORD, and rejecters of HIS provision of deliverance of salvation, in and through the Blood of JESUS CHRIST!

Including those in heaven, all on earth and those who have died not believing in THE LIGHT of THE WORLD JESUS CHRIST as their SAVIOR and LORD!

14

Work out your own salvation

Philippians 2:12-18, -

"Therefore, my beloved brethren, as you have always obeyed, not as in my presence only, but now much more in my absence, work out your own salvation with fear and trembling; for it is GOD WHO works in you both to will and to do for HIS good pleasure. Do all things without complaining and disputing, that you may become blameless and harmless, children of GOD without fault in the midst of a crooked and perverse generation, among whom you shine as lights in the world, holding fast THE WORD of LIFE, so that I may rejoice in the Day of CHRIST that I have not run in vain or labored in vain. Yes, and I am being poured out as a drink offering on the sacrifice and service of your faith, I am glad and rejoice with you all. For the same reason you also be glad and rejoice with me."

"Work out your own salvation with fear and trembling."

This does not mean that we are to seek to earn salvation, as your salvation was, "A Gift from ALMIGHTY GOD! Nor is it to work seeking rewards, O No!

Rather strongly stating that born-again Christians are to - 'work, the daily 'Out Flow' - 'As in exhibiting'
The Truth that is now within their inner most being. Your work (performance), your daily life is the way, the method of living out, the Living SPIRIT of GOD within! In your daily walk the inner life is to be seen – thus working out, presenting your SAVIOR WHO dwells within of your salvation!

As it is, ALMIGHTY GOD WHO dwells within you, WHO is ministering in and through you for HIS Glory, Plans and Purposes!

Christians (former old man) natural hearts, souls, mind, spirit and wills, have been re-created. Old things have been passed away. As we are now to 'put on the new man created in CHRIST JESUS!'

This is the 'exhibiting work' that we are to present, - to this, unfortunately, "Crooked and perverse nation (generation), among whom we – "Are to shine as lights."

Shining brightly enough that the lost in this perverse generation may see, the 'way out of the darkness' of their despair!

Please note that this does not apply only to the leaders of the Truth, as pastors, teachers, evangelists, elders and so forth. No, - It applies to each and every one of us born-again Christians. And regardless to your individual, 'state' of being a brand new Christian or a fully mature one.

We are to *"Work out"* as in presenting, demonstrating with our very lives – as it where in *"Fear and Trembling"* as Christians are "Ambassadors for CHRIST!"

2 Corinthians 5:19-21, - *That is,* -
"That GOD was in CHRIST reconciling the world to HIMSELF, not imputing their trespasses to them, and has committed to us the word of reconciliation. Now then we are ambassadors for CHRIST, as though GOD were pleading through us: we implore you on CHRIST'S behalf, be reconciled to GOD. For HE made HIM WHO knew no sin to be sin for us, that we might become the righteousness of GOD in HIM."

And if you are a born-again Christian, it does not matter, if you are a very young believer, -

2:13, *"For it is GOD WHO works in you both to will and to do for HIS good pleasure."*

This presenting (demonstrating – work) is not of us, but our LORD GOD ministering in and through us for HIS honor and glory!

However, we are to be as *"Children of GOD"* children meaning, obedient to THE FATHER! Earthly children reflect their family, demonstrating how they were brought up and the values they were taught, as well their culture. We being children of ALMIGHTY GOD, are to reflect that culture and go forth, blameless and harmless as THE LORD'S begotten children, without fault testifying to this crooked and perverse generation, who so desperately needs to not only hear it, but become GOD'S children also escaping the horrible wrath to come during the terrible Tribulation (Rev. Chapters 6-19).

Philippians Verse 2:17, *"... I am being poured out as a drink offering on the sacrifice and service of your faith, I am glad and rejoice with you all."*

That is the definition of, 'Work out your salvation'. Our Christian lives are to be as an, 'Offering, a sacrifice of faith' being poured forth, fearful of nothing, but in all things waiting and depending on ALMIGHTY GOD for your daily needs as you so go forth!

Knowing, whatever happens, or takes place, it is 'All Known' to THE LORD GOD' WHO is watching over you! And deeply cares for you!

15

All seek their own

Philippians 2:19-24, -

"But I trust in THE LORD JESUS to send Timothy to you shortly, that I also may be encouraged when I know your state. For I have no one like-minded, who will sincerely care for your state for all seek their own, not the things of CHRIST JESUS. But you know his proven character, that as a son with his father he served with me in the gospel. Therefore I hope to send him at once, as soon as I see how it goes with me. But I trust in THE LORD that I myself shall also come shortly."

> *"For all seek their own, not the things of CHRIST JESUS."*

Not so with Timothy, who was brought up in the faith, mentored by none other than the apostle Paul, therefore, young Timothy's mind is, CHRIST centered as his spiritual father Paul.

We are considering this epistle to the Philippians as a devotional. Then what can we learn from this? To apply, GOD'S WORD to our lives and grow spiritually and avoid, the self-seeking of the natural man and to maintain a walk with our LORD GOD?

Merely being wise in the historical facts, regardless of there being good or not, does not give light to our path. THE WORD of GOD is for us that we may grow in our knowledge and understanding, of our LORD and – 'apply' it into our inner most beings, our heart, soul, mind, spirit and will.

THE HOLY SPIRIT has made known to us, in 2:21 that we are not to place our lives or our concerns ahead of THE LORD JESUS CHRIST.

>But put CHRIST first!

The rebuke in verse 21 is, *"they seek their own, not the things which are of CHRIST JESUS."* Earlier, it was stated, *"some preach CHRIST from selfish ambition, not sincerely, supposing to add to my afflictions ..."*

Then in verse 2:20, *"I have no one like-minded, who will sincerely care for you ..."*

Another giant of the faith, Elijah in 1 Kings 19:10, *"I alone am left."* THE LORD answers in 1 Kings 19:18, *"Yet I have reserved seven thousand (7,000) in Israel, all whose knees have not bowed to baal, and every mouth that has not kissed him."*

We are not to judge others. As their cultures may differ from ours. I recall a story of two German pastors, talking about pastors in the United States.

They were talking to each other about the ones in the U.S. how could they possibly be Christians, as they wear such outlandish neck ties? The one smoking a cigar turned and responded to the one who was smoking a cigarette ...

Do All Things Through Christ

The apostle Paul being kept a prisoner for a number of years, is a bit discouraged that none of the others were willing to travel all the way to Philippi to strengthen and encourage them there.

However, even if the others are 'out of fellowship' with THE LORD, there is a way back for each of us.

The Old Testament is filled with examples and here is but one.

Bible readers know how sinful, disobedient and not seeking THE LORD GOD was the most wicked king of Israel, Ahab.

1 Kings 16:30, *"Now Ahab the son of Omri did evil in the sight of THE LORD, more than any before him."*

He even took as his wife, the wicked Jezebel and they both worshipped baal in the temple of Baal.

However, our example is this. Regardless of where you are spiritually, - even defeated and out of touch, you may 'still' be re-united with THE LORD! Or if not saved, may be shown the Greatness and Glory of THE LORD, wherein, you may seek and turn to THE LORD!

Read the story of the wicked king Ahab in 1 kings 16:29 on to 20:28, here is just verse 20:28, -

"Thus says THE LORD; because the Syrians have said, "THE LORD is GOD of the hills, but HE is not GOD of the valleys," therefore I will deliver all this great multitude into your hand, and you shall know that IAM THE LORD."

Great circumstances of difficulties may be upon you, but, regardless of where you were, if (if) you turn back (return) change your direction, seeking THE LORD. HE can deliver you from even a vast great multitude, that you may –

'Know that HE THE LORD is GOD!'

16

Little known man of faith

Philippians 2:25-30, -

"Yet I considered it necessary to send to you Epaphroditus, my brother, fellow worker, and fellow soldier, but your messenger and the one who ministered to my need; since he was longing for you all, and was distressed because you had heard that he was sick. For indeed he was sick almost unto death; but GOD had mercy on him, and not only him but on me also, lest I should have sorrow upon sorrow. Therefore I sent him the more eagerly, that when you see him again you may rejoice, and I be less sorrowful. Receive him therefore in THE LORD with all gladness, and hold such in esteem; because for the work of CHRIST he came close to death, not regarding his life, to supply what was lacking in your service toward me."

The apostle Paul wanted to go himself. But being restricted to chains in Rome, he would send Timothy. Knowing on his return, Paul would feel as if he had been there, being Timothy was so, like-minded as Paul.

We also need to note, that Philippi is some 4 to 5 weeks travel in the best of weather and conditions. More likely 6 to 8 weeks under normal circumstances. Depending on the wind etc. as it is some 800 miles distant from Rome.

THE SPIRIT intervenes, as the believers in Philippi were much concerned about the health and welfare of a special friend and loved one, Epaphroditus (as he was one of them).

Paul being obedient to THE SPIRIT sends Epaphroditus for he was as concerned for the believers in Philippi as they for him.

THE HOLY SPIRIT has an open field to minister in and through us, when (only when) self is set aside and fully surrendered to THE LORD of GLORY.

This is the meaning of Galatians 2:20, -

"I have been crucified with CHRIST; it is no longer I who live, but CHRIST lives in me; and the life which I now live in the flesh I live by faith in THE SON of GOD, WHO loved me and gave HIMSELF for me."

We can be self-centered, seeking our own ways and not after CHRIST. Or release ourselves into the Hands of ALMIGHTY GOD!

I am sure you fully realize which hands are the best to be kept in, as our LORD'S Hands reach out 'to and through all eternity.'

Now about Epaphroditus, in verse 2:30, he is referred to as the one who at risk to his very life, brought the supply (info on prayers, funds, food, etc.) from the believers at Philippi to Rome for Paul use in his on-going ministry there.

Did you know of Epaphroditus, before this? Here in Philippians is the only place that he is mentioned. Some scholars suggest that Epaphras, is a shortened name for Epaphroditus. While many others disagree. Since Epaphroditus is fully spelled out here in this short epistle, why was his name shortened in the others. Therefore, this is the only mention of this great man of the faith.
THE HOLY SPIRIT is reaching out to us, making it known, that we as individuals are not what is important, but JESUS CHRIST and the gospel Truth about HIM is!
As THE SPIRIT has recorded for us down through the centuries of this little known man of great faith and work (ministry) to others. Declaring that he is a man of faith, known for being a –

Brother of deep faith as the apostle Paul –
- Fellow worker
- Fellow soldier
- Messenger

Apparently he was a special man of faith back in his home assembly at Philippi. As he was sent, fully knowing that he would travel the great distance and their supply would be truthfully and faithfully presented to the apostle Paul in chains in Rome.

He was known by Paul as well the Christians in Philippi as a worker (minister) of the faith. Presenting the Truths of JESUS CHRIST as often as he possibly could.

A fellow soldier, setting aside his life desires as soldiers do. Then putting his life at risk, being a fellow believer amongst hostile dis-believers. And then going-forth, among and thru them.

A special messenger – special being two ways special. Bringing news hope, funds supply and most importantly 'prayers' from the faithful, way back in Philippi. Now barely recovering from some deep sickness, he is anxious to return, less the believers back in Philippi become concerned and worried over his demise!

Therefore, in agreement with Paul, he sets out to return the long distance of 4 to 8 weeks of difficult travel to get back.

Returning to his beloved ones, with this letter of hope, thanks and prayer for them!

Question, 'for what' are we known –in our assembly?

17

Brethren Beware

Philippians 3:1-3, -

"Finally, my brethren, rejoice in THE LORD. For me to write the same things to you is not tedious, but for you it is safe. Beware of dogs, beware of evil workers, beware of the mutilation! For we are the circumcision, who worship GOD in THE SPIRIT, rejoice in CHRIST JESUS, and have no confidence in the flesh."

In an attempt to make this more easily to be understood, here is the same passage in the Amplified Bible.

"For the rest, my brethren, delight yourselves in THE LORD and continue to rejoice that you are in HIM. To keep writing to you [over and over] of the same things is not irksome to me, and it is [a precaution] for your safety. Look out for those dogs [the Judaizers], look out for those mischief-workers, look out for those who mutilate the flesh. For we [Christians] are the true circumcision, who worship GOD in spirit and by THE SPIRIT of GOD, and exult and glory and pride ourselves in JESUS CHRIST, and put no confidence or dependence [on what we are] in the flesh and on outward privileges and physical advantages and external appearances."

End quote from Amplified Bible. Again the use of all capital letters about THE LORD GOD, are of HR.

Brethren beware, -
- Beware of dogs
- Beware of evil workers
- Beware of the mutilation

I am aware of one scholar, who declared that in those early days – wild dogs roamed in pacts freely and were a menace to the safety of mankind.

But that is not what THE SPIRIT is cautioning us about, physical wild dogs, no!

Unfortunately we see the very same thing going on today, in this our once great nation. The term, 'wild dogs roaming freely in pacts' describes the burning of cities, riots, looting of stores and public disturbance and disobedience to the 'laws of the land' that many today are engaged in! As they think that 'only their way' is the proper one. Sad isn't it? However, this describes the 'add on' teaching of the Judaizers and how disrupting they were in their presentations.

THE HOLY SPIRIT'S ministry through Paul, was directing Christians 'away from traditions, creeds and especially add-ons as the Judaizers.' Who insisted that before one could be saved, they had first to be circumcised.

Therefore, this group of 'add on' teachers fit into all three groups to be avoided. The dogs, evil workers and the mutilation.

And the remedy then is the very same today in 2017 on. Today, we must take a stand on the basic foundational Truths of JESUS CHRIST and the gospel. And not only to stand, but proclaim, teaching and admonishing, unless they believe in JESUS CHRIST for their salvation, they will perish is the fiery pit of hell!

And in so doing, we are not to exalt ourselves, rather just the very opposite as the man of faith, Epaphroditus.

18

May I Gain CHRIST

Philippians 3:4-6, - 3:7-11, -

"Though I also might have confidence in the flesh. If anyone else thinks he may have confidence in the flesh, I more so; circumcised the eighth day, of the stock of Israel, of the tribe of Benjamin, a Hebrew of the Hebrews; concerning the law, a Pharisee; concerning zeal, persecuting the church; concerning righteousness which is in the law, blameless."

If anyone thinks that he/she is 'above' because of their standing in a 'superior assembly' - that is their teaching is superior because, of the Bible version they use. Or their manner of dress (as they adhere exactly to the highest standards). The number of meetings held, and their rigid holding to certain, add on viewpoints of various doctrines. The chosen apostle Paul has even a deeper and broader standing, and THE SPIRIT has it spelled out, for us, in those verses 4 through 6.

Then providing the 'Foundational Truths of JESUS CHRIST' in verses 7 through 11.

Philippians 3:7-11, -

"But what things were gain to me, these I have counted as loss for CHRIST. Yet indeed I also count all things loss for the excellence of the knowledge of CHRIST JESUS my LORD, for WHOM I have suffered the loss of all things, and count them as rubbish, that I may gain CHRIST and be found in HIM, not having my own righteousness, which is from the law, but that which is through faith in CHRIST, the righteousness which is from GOD by faith; that I may know HIM and the power of HIS resurrection, and the fellowship of HIS sufferings, being conformed to HIS death, if, by any means, I may attain to the resurrection from the dead."

THE SPIRIT'S teaching here is, 'anything that you think sets you apart or somewhat above other brethren' – please know and understand this –

'Such so-called gain', = means, -
A "loss" for CHRIST!!

There are many if not most, consider their assembly far above others and fully expect the people in the community to come in because of who and what they are. And unfortunately many others consider it the job responsibility of 'the pastor' to bring them in. Then when the people do not come and some inside stop attending. Many times the reason for the departure of some is, there is a lack of love and concern for one another. People feel and sense, the coldness and the separate cliques who only gather with those in their clique, within that assembly, how sad.

Then because some leave and others do not come in, results in their asking the pastor to leave! Again, how sad. As they fail to realize that it is, **every Christian's**

responsibility to 'go-forth' proclaiming JESUS CHRIST. And doing so with united loving concern for one another inside and the lost outside.

The out-siders, seeing and sensing this union of deep love and concern, out-reaching into the community, respond and come to see what the reason is!

Of course the reason is – CHRIST in you!

Recently I have heard from a friend of mine about his daughter who is in her third year of college.

The note she sent to family and family friends is 'heartwarming' indeed. Here is but a sample, omitting her name and the large city in the East.

Partial (edited) quote –

'I had the opportunity to spend my Spring break with friends in a large city in the East. We spent the entire week sharing the gospel with students at other universities. One of my favorite experiences happened in an area where the purest and cheapest heroin could be found. We spent the afternoon handing out free lunches and hot coffee to the many people milling around on the corner. While handing out the lunches, we had conversations and heard many stories about how the people came to this city. We offered to pray for them. This was an awesome experience because everyone was so open to sharing their story with us and allowed us to pray for them.

This summer, I have the opportunity to take part in a summer mission. I will be joining with about fifteen other college students to spend three weeks in that large city. One group will be involved with outreaches on college campuses throughout the city and in the community. I will also be involved in a small group Bible study and one-on-one discipleship.

My heart's desire is to increase my understanding of GOD'S WORD, deepen my relationship with HIM, and be more burdened for reaching people with the gospel. I am very excited for this opportunity but I am also nervous because I know my faith will be stretched throughout this three week adventure.'

End of partial quote, capital letters for GOD, is HR

Wow! I was so excited to read this, as it sure 'Lifted me up' – perhaps there is hope for our once great country, if – If young people across our nation, become so excited and "Go Forth" with the good news of the gospel, as these young people, praise our LORD and may we pray for them to so do!

Philippians 3:8, "... *I have suffered the loss of all things, and count them as rubbish, that I may gain CHRIST."*

You and I consider the loss of all things as relating to 'things, personal property.' But Paul did not even mention that he 'Lost his Freedom' he was bond in chains and this for a number of years. However, this loss was viewed as merely the loss of things, that he might gain more of CHRIST! What does this 'Shout out' to the likes of you and me?

Philippians 3:10-11, -

"That I may know HIM and the power of HIS resurrection, and the fellowship of HIS sufferings, being conformed to HIS death, if by any means, I may attain to the resurrection from the dead."

This is what THE SPIRIT desires for us – that we know CHRIST and the power of HIS resurrection. Not merely in intellectual head knowledge, but in newness, demonstrated by a changed life! A life that puts on the 'new man in CHRIST' going forth with a glad and joyous heart, that reveals the new life within!

That is, being so identified with CHRIST, that HIS resurrected life would be implanted and seen in us! That our new life in HIM, would empower us to go forth, not turning aside, due to sufferings or difficulties. Our newness being raised from the dead life of sin, reveals as if we have been raised from the dead!

19

Press On for CHRIST

Philippians 3:12-16, -

"Not that I have already attained, or am already perfected; but I press on, that I may lay hold of that for which CHRIST JESUS has also laid hold of me. Brethren, I do not count myself to have apprehended; but one thing I do, forgetting those things which are behind and reaching forward to those things which are ahead. I press toward the goal for the prize of the upward call of GOD in CHRIST JESUS. Therefore let us, as many as are mature, have this mind; and if in anything you think otherwise, GOD will reveal even this to you. Nevertheless, to the degree that we have already attained, let us walk by the same rule, let us be of the same mind."

THE HOLY SPIRIT is reaching out here, bringing us 'down' from our thoughts of 'loftiness' where we thought we were.

Verse 15, THE SPIRIT, puts it very intensely, -

> *"As many as are mature, have this mind ..."*

If we consider that we are no longer babes in CHRIST, rather, mature, then THE SPIRIT is declaring this, in clear, easy to understand terms, *"Have this mind."*

The mind THE SPIRIT is speaking about is, -

"Not that I have already attained, or am perfected"

Regardless where you are in your, devotions, Bible study, or theological training, -

'You Have NOT Arrived' –

To the place, the level that ALMIGHTY GOD in CHRIST has called and chosen you to! No!

As it is not an obtainable, in this life. For in this life, we must ever be reaching forward, upward to the high calling that our LORD has chosen us to and for!

Ever seeking a greater abiding fellowship, relationship with THE LORD of our salvation.

THE HOLY SPIRIT is using the Apostle Paul's life as an illustration for us. As mature as Paul was, he had not arrived at the place, the calling that he was chosen for by his SAVIOR JESUS CHRIST!

The question is, what then of you and me? Are we seeking to defend our position? Or are we going to be obedient to THE SPIRIT?

And do as it is written in verse 13, -

"Forgetting those things which are behind and reaching forward to those things which are ahead."

We cannot do anything about yesterday. Today is the tomorrow of yesterday. Therefore, may we reach forward ever seeking new heights via searching after new lives to witness and testify to, giving them assurance of eternal glory that is only available in, CHRIST JESUS, THE LORD of GLORY!

THE SPIRIT of GOD, is greatly encouraging us in verse 14. Using Paul's life as an example. Regardless of the lofty place where he was spiritually, -

"Press toward the goal for the prize of the upward call of GOD –
"In CHRIST JESUS."

O may we so do, ever stretching and reaching upward to a loftier goal, 'In CHRIST.'

"Let us walk by the same rule, let us be of the same mind."

20

Stand Fast in THE LORD

Philippians 3:17-4:1, -

"Brethren, join in following my example, and note those who so walk, as you have us for a pattern. For many walk, of whom I have told you often, and now tell you even weeping, that they are the enemies of the Cross of CHRIST: Whose end is destruction, whose god is their belly, and whose glory is their shame – who set their mind on earthly things. For our citizenship is in heaven, from which we also eagerly wait for THE SAVIOR, THE LORD JESUS CHRIST, WHO will transform our lowly body that it may be conformed to HIS Glorious Body, according to the working by which HE is able to subdue all things to HIMSELF. Therefore, my beloved and longed – for brethren, my joy and crown, so stand fast in THE LORD beloved."

Verse 19, is from 18, -

"The enemies of the cross of CHRIST."

Then vs. 19, *"Whose end is destruction ..."*

Those who mind earthly things unfortunately are set – heading headlong into destruction! And are seen as enemies of Christianity.

The born-again believers hope is, "In CHRIST" and verse 21 clearly sets forth, -

"HE is able even to subdue all things to HIMSELF."

Whatever, your circumstances, regardless of your concern, *"Stand Fast in THE LORD JESUS CHRIST."*

As HE is able to *"Subdue all things to HIMSELF."*

THE LORD is able to subdue any and all things to HIMSELF, for HE is THE CREATOR and THE SUSTAINER of all things!

So whatever is taking place in your life, it has been permitted by THE LORD of GLORY, for HIS Plans and HIS Purposes in and with you.

Those who know me or have read my books, also know that I am a reader of "My Utmost for HIS Highest" by Oswald Chambers, a daily devotional. Mine, is an old one (60 years), it was given to me by my mentor, Mr. Bart Hargreaves a few days after leading me to believing faith in JESUS CHRIST as my SAVIOR and LORD!

Here is the devotional from April the 13th. Quote –

"What to do under the Conditions"

"Cast thy burden upon THE LORD." Psalm 55:22
We must distinguish between the burden-bearing that is right and the burden-bearing that is wrong. We ought never to bear the burden of sin or of doubt, but there are burdens placed on us by GOD which HE does not intend

to lift off, HE wants us to roll them back on HIM. "Cast that HE hath given thee upon THE LORD." (R.V. marg.) If we undertake work for GOD and get out of touch with HIM, the sense of responsibility will be overwhelmingly crushing; but if we roll back on GOD that which HE has put on us, HE takes away the sense of responsibility by bringing in the realization of HIMSELF. Many workers have gone out with high courage and fine impulses, but with no intimate fellowship with JESUS CHRIST, and before long they are crushed, they do not know what to do with the burden, it produces weariness, and the people say – "What an embittered end to such a beginning!" "Roll thy burden upon THE LORD" – you have been bearing it all; deliberately put one end on the shoulders of GOD. The government shall be upon HIS shoulder." Commit to GOD that HE hath given thee"; not fling it off, but put it over on to HIM and yourself with it, and the burden is lightened by the sense of companionship. Never disassociate yourself from the burden."

End quote, use of capital letters of, for GOD - HR

Question, who do you imitate in your walk? THE SPIRIT uses the life example of Paul as a good one. Also referring perhaps to his close associates, Timothy and Epaphroditus as excellent examples to follow after.

Amos 3:3, *"Can two walk together, unless they are agreed?"*

To walk together, they 'must have the same destination.' If ones desire is to Jerusalem and the other Jericho, they cannot walk together as their destinations are in the opposite direction.

Unfortunately that is one of the major problems in today's assemblies, walking together. As some –

Desire is to have more attendees
Some to have a larger building
Some demand, their versions of doctrine only
Some seek merely a clique of followers

The list of things that divide us seems to sadly grow. Is this what THE SPIRIT was teaching and warning about? That such, are enemies of the Cross of CHRIST who mind earthly things. For our citizenship is in heaven.

Our walk together, should be – to be like CHRIST!

THE HOLY SPIRIT, puts it this way in Colossians 2:5-6, *"For though I am absent in the flesh, yet I am with you in spirit, rejoicing to see your good order and the steadfastness of your faith in CHRIST. As you therefore have received CHRIST JESUS THE LORD, so walk in HIM."*

Thus we are to, 'Walk in Faith' the same faith that drew us and we believed in HIM.

Our mind as well our hearts are to be ever looking Up-Ward to the sudden appearing of our SAVIOR and LORD in the clouds to 'Rapture us up' – into Heaven's Glory and that for all eternity! We dwell here as 'aliens' for we (born-again Christians) are citizens of Heaven's Glory.

And on the 'Up-Ward journey' (in an instant) we will be changed, transformed from our lowly bodies, being conformed into Heavenly bodies.

Remember, whatever we face, what circumstances we endure, our LORD GOD is able to *"Subdue all things to HIMSELF."*

4:1, *"Therefore, my beloved and longed – for brethren, my joy and crown, so stand fast in THE LORD, beloved."*

21

THE LORD is at hand

Philippians 4:2-7, -

"I implore Euodia and I implore Syntyche to be of the same mind in THE LORD. And I urge you also, true companion, help these women who labored with me in the gospel, with Clement also, and the rest of my fellow workers, whose names are in the Book of Life. Rejoice in THE LORD always. Again I will say, rejoice! Let your gentleness be known to all men. THE LORD is at hand. Be anxious for nothing, but in everything by prayer and supplication, with thanksgiving, let your requests be made known to GOD; and the peace of GOD, which surpasses all understanding, will guard your hearts and minds through CHRIST JESUS."

Verse 5, sets the stage for all workers and their ministry. Their walking together towards the very same destination and their abiding union with one another.

"THE LORD is at hand."

Praise ALMIGHTY GOD, yes, THE LORD is at hand as HE may appear at any moment in the clouds with a shout, the voice of an angel and the sounding of a trumpet!

Another giant, the Apostle James, is the vessel THE SPIRIT used to give us – James 5:7-9, -

"Therefore be patient, brethren, until the coming of THE LORD. See how the farmer waits for the precious fruit of the earth, waiting patiently for it until it receives the early and latter rain. You also be patient. Establish your hearts, for the coming of THE LORD is at hand. Do not grumble against one another, brethren, lest you be condemned. Behold, THE JUDGE is standing at the door!"

Yes, beloved ones, remember THE JUDGE of all the earth and those dwelling therein, is at the door beholding as we go-forth and, if and when we remain refusing!

Here in Philippians 4:5-7, is THE SPIRIT'S message through Paul, not only to the two women noted in verse 2, but 'to all the fellow workers whose names are in the Book of Life.'

Two highly regarded women of faith, Euodia and Syntyche had some disagreement. THE HOLY SPIRIT implores them to be of the same mind. That is agree and be fully united with each other. For nothing in this life is as valuable as ones citizenship in Heaven's Glory! Then THE SPIRIT instructs all whose names are in the Book of Life to also step forward and assist these precious ladies in togetherness!

THE SPIRIT'S message to all whose names are in the Book of Life – including you and I, we are to be 'constantly rejoicing in THE LORD' and our gentleness is to be known and shown to all others. Doing so without being anxious over anything. Instead, be ever earnestly in deep prayer and thanksgiving for all – informing THE LORD of your concerns and asking, seeking that, 'HIS will be done!' Turning everything over to THE LORD, then the peace of GOD will flow in and through you to those in need.

22

Meditate on these things

Philippians 4:8-9, -

"Finally, brethren, whatever things are true, whatever things are noble, whatever things are just, whatever things are pure, whatever things are lovely, whatever things are of good report, if there is any virtue and if there is anything praiseworthy – meditate on these things. The things which you learned and received and heard and saw in me, these do, and THE GOD of Peace will be with you."

What a message from THE SPIRIT, 'Meditate on the things that are praise worthy.' As we are not to be concerned about yesterday, nor the things thereof. They are behind and beyond any reach. If they were acts of unkindness, then confess, make restitution, seeking forgiveness and move ahead.

If they were acts of unkindness against you, respond quickly, 'giving forgiveness' and restoring sweet fellowship together.

Question, what do others see in us? As the things seen in Paul's life, heard from his testimony the Philippians were to copy, and follow after.

Has or will THE SPIRIT, seek to have others follow after our walk, our testimony, our example of the witnessing and proclamation of the gospel?

These are the things that we are to meditate on. Things that are –

True – noble – just – pure – lovely – good report

These are to be found, in 'abundance' with born-again Christians who are abiding in JESUS CHRIST and HIS WORDS abiding in them.

The word, meditate means = to reflect upon, ponder. To plan or intend in the mind. To engage in contemplation. That is to exercise a plan, not merely thinking of them, but develop a course of action that brings the things worthy of meditation into and being part of our lives.

Christians who so develop and make these as part of their lives will be rewarded –

> *"THE GOD of PEACE will be with you!"*

23

Do all things through CHRIST

Philippians 4:10-14, -

"But I rejoiced in THE LORD greatly that now at last your care for me has flourished again; though you surely did care, but you lacked opportunity. Not that I speak in regard to need, for I have learned in whatever state I am, to be content: I know how to be abased, and I know how to abound. Everywhere and in all things I have learned both to be full and to be hungry, both to abound and to suffer need. I can do all things through CHRIST WHO strengthens me. Nevertheless you have done well that you shared in my distress.

"I can do all things through CHRIST WHO strengthens me."

THE HOLY SPIRIT did not reveal this at the very beginning, no, but left it here for those who are seeking an on-going abiding fellowship with THE LORD of GLORY JESUS CHRIST! On-going is continuing to learn, asking and seeking THE SPIRIT'S guidance in Deeping your walk with THE LORD.

This is available to those who are seeking wisdom and knowledge of THE LORD. As the Scriptures declare – Proverbs 1:2-7, -

"To know wisdom and instruction, to perceive the words of understanding, to receive the instruction of wisdom, justice, judgment, and equity; to give prudence to the simple, to the young man knowledge and discretion – A wise man will hear and increase in learning, and a man of understanding will attain wise counsel, to understand a proverb and an enigma, the words of the wise and their riddles. The Fear of THE LORD is the beginning of knowledge, but fools despise wisdom and instruction."

"The Fear of THE LORD is the beginning ..."

This means, reverential trust in THE LORD. Belief and worshipping HIM, WHO created you and is now sustaining you.

Proverbs 9:10, -

"The Fear of THE LORD is the beginning of wisdom, and knowledge of THE HOLY ONE is understanding."

Proverbs 14:26, -

"In the Fear of THE LORD there is strong confidence, and HIS children will have a place of refuge. The Fear of THE LORD is a fountain of life, to turn away from the snares of death."

Therefore, beloved ones in CHRIST we need, we must continue on in seeking knowledge of our LORD, that we may be HIS ministers in this –
'Dark perverted age'
That we now find ourselves in.

As our only hope, our only confidence is in JESUS CHRIST, WHO created all things. HE is able to subdue all things. As all things have been already placed under HIS feet by ALMIGHTY GOD THE FATHER!

Born-again Christians are to be in, reverential trust, belief and worshipping THE LORD GOD of our creation, then continuing on seeking full knowledge of HIM through HIS HOLY WORD, then, only then, we can rejoice in, -

"I can do all things through CHRIST WHO strengthens me."

Being so strengthened we may go-forth in full confidence, as THE SPIRIT has relayed to us the life and ministry of HIS servant Paul.

Everything was not, as we say, 'peaches and cream,' sometimes servants are hungry and suffer lack. However, our lives are not measured by the abundance 'of things' no. Rather in our relationship our abiding union, our believing fellowship with THE AWESOME LORD of GLORY!

And unfortunately, most unfortunately we do not seek fellowship with THE LORD, when things are going well and we are in abundance of things.

But when things are lacking, or health is failing, we cry out, and continue crying until we receive assistance and or deliverance.

And such is clearly stated here in Philippians 4:10-13 and on. As the giant in faith Paul suffered lack. But his response was, 'on-going with THE LORD.' Things nor happenings are not to deter us from our ministry of belief, and gaining fuller knowledge of our LORD.

THE SPIRIT clearly has demonstrated to us through the life of Paul, that we are to continue, 'Looking Up' permitting nothing to deter or separate us from our believing faith in WHO JESUS CHRIST is and WHO HE is, to each and every one of us!

"I can do all things through CHRIST WHO strengthens me."

24

Sweet – Smelling Aroma

Philippians 4:14-18, -

"Nevertheless you have done well that you shared in my distress. Now you Philippians know also that in the beginning of the gospel, when I departed from Macedonia, no church shared with me concerning giving and receiving but you only. For even in Thessalonica you sent aid once and again for my necessities. Not that I seek the gift, but I seek the fruit that abounds in your account. Indeed I have all and abound. I am full, having received from Epaphroditus the things sent by you, a sweet - smelling aroma, and acceptable sacrifice, well pleasing to GOD.

"A sweet - smelling aroma, and acceptable sacrifice, well pleasing to GOD."

O beloved, is this how we are seen and known? Especially to our LORD GOD, WHO redeemed us?

Or, are we as, 'no church shared with me concerning giving and receiving.' What a strong rebuke, *'no church concerned with giving.'*

None sharing, results in always lacking. Never seeming to have enough to meet every day needs. Is this because they have not, 'put GOD first?'

When we share the gospel as well funds, for others to go-forth sharing the good news, this 'is fruit' that abounds to our account in Glory.

The prophet Haggai speaks to this very point in Haggai 1:2-7, - King James Version –

"Thus speaketh THE LORD of HOSTS, saying, this people say the time is not come, the time THE LORD'S House should be built. Then came THE WORD of THE LORD by Haggai the prophet, saying, is it time for you, O ye, to dwell in your ceiled houses, and this house lie waste? Now therefore thus saith THE LORD of HOSTS; consider your ways. Ye have sown much, and bring in little, ye eat, but ye have not enough; ye drink, but ye are not filled with drink; ye clothe you, but there is none warm; and he that earneth wages to put into a bag with holes. Thus saith THE LORD consider your ways.

Look at it this way – THE LORD'S house as being our relationship in and with HIM.

The ceiled house is our way, our life being as we desire it. Then leaving out, any on-going relationship with THE LORD.

Since some people put themselves first – 'living in ceiled houses and 'not having an abiding fellowship' with THE LORD. THE LORD has a strong rebuke for such ones!

Haggai 1:9-10, -

"Ye looked for much, and lo, it came to little; and when you brought it home I did blow upon it. Why? Saith THE LORD of HOSTS. Because of MINE house that is in waste, and ye run

every man unto his house. Therefore the heaven over you is stayed from dew, and the earth is stayed from her fruit."

A Christian may be employed and receive decent wages, but, but if there is no on-going abiding union together with THE LORD, his, wages seem to be constantly going into a bag with holes, as there is never enough!

And if the lack of fellowship is so severe, THE LORD may even blow on what he does have and it is gone. Leaving him desperately struggling – then, then he may cry out to THE LORD asking and seeking HIS assistance. But first he must re-establish his union with his HEAVENLY FATHER. And this may be but a beginning of a long, testing road of return.

But praise our LORD GOD, that a 'Return is Possible' and HIS Arms are out-stretched still, ready to embrace any seeking to 'Re-Build THE LORD'S house within themselves.'

That is the 'Inner Sanctuary' where THE HOLY SPIRIT dwells. 1 Corinthians 3:16, - KJV

"Know ye not that ye are the Temple of GOD, and that THE SPIRIT of GOD dwelleth in you?"

And in this re-established union, and on-going fellowship with THE LORD, one may again be a –
"Sweet smelling aroma" – well pleasing to GOD!

25

Your Needs Supplied

Philippians 4:19, -

"And my GOD shall supply all your need according to HIS riches in glory by CHRIST JESUS."

To those who are as a 'Sweet Smelling Aroma' an acceptable sacrifice, well pleasing to GOD will have all their needs met, with the limitations being, -

"According to HIS Riches in Glory by CHRIST JESUS."

Therefore, without any earthly measure!

Wow! Instead of bringing home wages in a bag with holes, or having THE LORD GOD blow them away. THE LORD, will pour forth, from HIS vast riches in Glory to those who are in an on-going, abiding union (fellowship, relationship) with THE LORD, their SAVIOR!

Philippians 4:22 is very enlightening, -

"All the saints greet you, but especially those who are of Caesar's household."

Think of it, Paul is a prisoner of Caesar and in chains and guarded daily and throughout the night. In chains because of his witness and testimony of WHO JESUS CHRIST is! As he faithfully proclaimed JESUS CHRIST as the PROMISED ONE, THE DELIVER from sin, ushering believers into citizens of heaven!

But in spite of his chains and the constant guards, the household servants of Caesar have come to know CHRIST as their SAVIOR?!!

What then, can we claim is the reason we do not go-forth? I recently asked a church goer, if he would consider being part of an Evangelistic Team, to hold Evangelistic meetings once a summer? His answer, "I am busy."

Greet every saint in CHRIST JESUS, now to our GOD and FATHER be glory forever, the grace of our LORD JESUS CHRIST be with you all. Amen.

Other books by Howard Rudolph

"Twice Born" – a life story of redemption

"Lead me in the Way Everlasting" – Biblical studies of various subjects and doctrines

"Continue in the Faith" – biblical studies going forth

"A Full Reward be given thee of THE LORD" – a biblical study and application of the Old Testament book of Ruth

"A Chosen Servant's Walk" – a devotional on the 24th chapter of Genesis, a wife for Isaac

"The Hour is Coming" – a devotional study seeking to awaken us from our 'lethargic sleep'

"I Will Not Have You to be Ignorant Brethren" – a devotional bible study concerning the events of 'The Latter Days' including the Rapture – meeting THE LORD in the air, the Judgment Seat of CHRIST and the terrible Tribulation

"The Way, The Truth and The Life" – a devotional bible study of JESUS CHRIST stating that HE is – The Way, The Truth, and The Life. John 14:1-6

"Our Confidence Steadfast to the End" – a devotional biblical bible study and exhortation for Christians to 'Remain Steadfast to the End'

"The Tabernacle as a Pattern for Christians" – a devotional on 1 Peter 2:9-10, you are chosen, a royal priesthood

"<u>Things which must shortly take place</u>" – a devotional study of the events leading up to the Tribulation and 'the book of Revelation'

"<u>Three Crosses at Calvary</u>" – a biblical study about two thieves and THE LORD of glory

"<u>Two Equals One</u>" – a devotional about marriage

"<u>Are You a Chosen One</u>" – a devotional about your calling, your salvation, your going forth

"<u>Triumphant in the Riches of GOD'S Grace</u>" – a devotional Bible study of the epistle known as Ephesians

"<u>The Abiding Life</u>" – a devotional Bible study of John 15:1-8

"<u>JESUS Began to Do and Teach</u>" – devotionals on the book of Acts

"<u>THE WORD OF GOD, is the FOUNTAIN of TRUTH</u>" – devotions for you to draw Life Supporting Nourishment from. Centered around Psalm 91

These books are available through
LULU.com

www.ingramcontent.com/pod-product-compliance
Lightning Source LLC
Chambersburg PA
CBHW031409040426
42444CB00005B/489